102 ESL Games an(... Kids

ESL Activities for Children

By Miles Jaworski

Copyright © Miles Jaworski 2015 The author asserts the moral right to be identified as the author of this work. All rights reserved. No part of this book may be reproduced or transmitted in any form or by any means, electronic, mechanical, photocopying or otherwise, without the prior written permission of the author.

Other books by this author

102 ESL Games and Activities for New and Prospective Teachers

Basic English Grammar: A Guide for New and Prospective ESL Teachers

English Grammar Exercises: A Complete Guide to English Tenses for ESL Students

Table of Contents

0. Introduction
1. Volleyball (vocabulary)
2. Chicken fights (vocabulary)
3. Name chairs (learning classmates' names)
4. Piggy in the middle (vocabulary)
5. Medina (numbers / bargaining / money)
6. What's your name? (what's you name? / my name is..)
7. Fingers on the buzzer (spelling)
8. Pin the tail on the donkey (prepositions / directions)
9. Blind student hunt (directions / listening)
10. What's the time, Mr Wolf? (telling time / numbers)
11. Question catch (question forms)
12. Vocabulary chairs (listening)
13. Treasure hunt (prepositions of place)
14. Answer me! (question forms / sentence structure)
15. Last letter first (vocabulary / spelling)
16. Student sentences (sentence structure / vocabulary)
17. Word hopscotch (vocabulary / pronunciation)
18. Riddle me this (writing / listening / speaking)

19. How are you feeling? (Feelings vocabulary)

20. Steady heads (vocabulary / imperatives / listening)

21. Countdown (vocabulary / spelling)

22. A day at the races (past simple / present perfect)

23. Spin the bottle (fluency)

24. As…..as……. (comparisons)

25. Parts of speech elimination (listening / parts of speech)

26. Lip reading (vocabulary)

27. Take a pace forwards if you… (listening)

28. Blind man's questions (listening / question forms)

29. Play time (writing)

30. What's the question? (question forms / tenses)

31. Airplane quiz (various)

32. Vocabulary race (vocabulary / reading)

33. Can you ball (can you..? questions and answers)

34. Wastepaper bin basketball (revision / various)

35. Alphabet statues (letters / the alphabet)

36. Play dough numbers and letters (numbers / letters)

37. Body swatting (body parts vocabulary)

38. Past tense pelmanism (past simple)

39. Question quiz (question forms)

40. Word fetch (vocabulary / listening / reading)

41. Animal mime (animal vocabulary)

42. Reading race (reading / listening / writing)

43. Who has it? (question forms / describing people)

44. What's this mingle (vocabulary / contractions)

45. What's missing flashcards (vocabulary / pronunciation)

46. Your joking! (reading / jokes)

47. Words worms (vocabulary)

48. Describe it! (vocabulary / describing things)

49. Reported speech ball toss (reported speech)

50. I don't agree! (fluency)

51. Last day word hunt (vocabulary review / scan reading)

52. Show me the time (telling time)

53. Three part sentences (reading / listening)

54. Vocabulary battle ship (vocabulary / spelling)

55. Animal heads (yes / no questions and answers)

56. Card sentences (sentence structure)

57. Alphabet Tracing (letters / the alphabet)

58. Musical words (vocabulary / reading)

59. Duck duck goose (vocabulary / pronunciation)

60. Preposition commands (listening / prepositions of place)

61. True / false line (vocabulary / pronunciation)

62. Spelling bee (spelling)

63. How are you? (everyday questions and answers)

64. Close your eyes (question forms)

65. Yes / no picture cards (yes / no questions)

66. Minimal pairs bingo (listening)

67. Please listen to me (listening / imperatives)

68. Dice lottery (various / revision)

69. Can you remember? (vocabulary)

70. Question circle (question forms)

71. Describe your classmates (describing people)

72. Story time (Sentence structure / parts of speech)

73. Preposition race (prepositions / listening)

74. Word morphing (vocabulary)

75. Seven things (vocabulary)

76. Student sit down (listening / responding0

77. Past, present or future (time phrases / fluency)

78. Slow motion reveal (vocabulary)

79. That's not true! (various / fluency)

80. Whacky races (action verbs)

81. Train ride (action verbs)

82. Code words (spelling / numbers)

83. Dominoes (the alphabet)

84. Snap-shot hunt (vocabulary)

85. ABC Song (the alphabet)

86. Stand up letters (letters / the alphabet)

87. Stand Up conditionals (conditionals / if clauses)

88. Tic tac toe pictures (vocabulary)

89. Follow the leader (action verbs)

90. Kabaddi tasks (various)

91. Article Challenge (articles)

92. Traffic Lights! (listening / imperatives)

93. Mannequin (clothes vocabulary)

94. Have I made a mistake? (various)

95. Holiday time (going to / present continuous)

96. Alphabet catch (the alphabet)

97. Would I lie to you? (present perfect / various)

98. Chinese whispers with a twist (listening / vocabulary)

99. Stop Boasting (fluency)

100. Good sentence, bad sentence (listening / grammar)

101. Musical objects (fluency)

102. Name lines (listening / learning classmates' names)

Introduction

Teaching English to children can be very rewarding. A properly motivated and well-managed class can learn at an astonishing rate, soaking up vocabulary and grammar with ease.

It can also, however, be tough, very tough. The short attention spans of younger students mean that they can become easily distracted. In addition, the younger your students, the less likely they are to have any intrinsic desire or motivation to learn English.

For these reasons, it is important to include a variety of fun, communicative activities and games in each and every lesson. These games and activities provide much needed motivation and ensure your students develop their language skills quickly and efficiently. They also help make conducting a young learners' class, enjoyable and stress-free.

I suggest you use the games and activities in this book liberally, as coolers, warmers and at any other stage of the lesson when you sense your students may becoming distracted or bored.

When setting up any of the games or activities, remember to show your students what to do, rather than tell them. It is far, far better to choose some of your more advanced, or confident, students to help demonstrate an activity than to embark on lengthy explanations that may only leave your students confused.

And finally, try not to give feedback to your students while they are engaged in an activity or game. Better to wait until the activity is over and to provide full-class feedback.

I hope you and your class enjoy this book!

1. Volleyball

Language / Skill practiced: Vocabulary

Time: 20 minutes

Language level: Beginner to intermediate

Really fun. You need a balloon, which you can ask one of you students to blow up. Now convert you classroom into a volleyball court by constructing a simple, "net" made of tables and chairs across the middle of the room. Divide the class into two teams, one each side of the net and pick a category, such as colors, animals, past participles or any other category of vocabulary you'd like to practice. Now begin the game! Each time a player hits the ball he must say a word from the category; only three hits on one side of the net allowed; if the balloon hits the floor, or a player doesn't say a a word correctly, the other team gains one point.

Keep a few balloons spare; things can get excitable!

2. Chicken fights

Language / Skill practiced: Vocabulary

Time: 5 minutes

Language level: Beginner / elementary

Pair up your students. Move tables and chairs to the side, away from the arena, or ring. Bring a pair to the front, stand them face to face, and stick a picture flashcard to the back of each student containing vocabulary you wish to practice. Now begin: each student must try to see what flashcard the other student has on her back. The first chicken – sorry student – to see her opponent's flash card and call out the word, wins. A very entertaining game which the kids seem to enjoy. You can have a knock out competition if you wish, or just play it for fun.

3. Name chairs

Language / Skill practiced: Learning classmates' names

Time: 5 to 10 minutes

Language level: Beginner to advanced

This is a great little game for the first day of class.

Arrange the students, and yourself, in chairs in a circle. Ask everyone, in turn, to say their names. When everyone has said their names, stand up and say the name of one of the students and move towards him. You are going to sit in his seat. This student should stand up and say the name of another student and move towards her to sit in her seat. This student should stand up and say the name of another student and so on and so on. Start out slow, but as the students become more familiar with their classmates' names, encourage a faster pace until students are jumping up and moving around at high speed.

4. Piggy in the middle

Language / Skill practiced: Vocabulary

Time: 10-15 minutes

Language level: Elementary to intermediate

Arrange your students in a circle. Pick one student to go in the middle. Announce a category such as, "Things in this classroom." Students throw a ball to each other, as in the traditional game, while the student in the middle tries to intercept the ball. However, each time a student catches the ball they must say a word from the category, such as "blackboard." If a student cannot think of a word, they become the "piggy." If the "piggy" intercepts the ball, the student who threw the ball becomes the "piggy."

5. Medina

Language / Skill practiced: Numbers / bargaining / money

Time: 25 minutes

Language level: Pre-intermediate to upper-intermediate

Demonstrate the concept of bargaining / haggling to you students. Also teach useful haggling vocabulary such as, "I'll take it," "How about…" "It's a deal," etc.

Divide the class into two halves. Give each student from one half of the class 50 dollars / pounds / euros in play money, in very small denominations. Give the other students five flashcards each, each one displaying an item that you might find in a market: fruit, socks, kitchenware – it doesn't really matter what the items are – and explain that each item is worth approximately the same amount of money.

Set a time limit of 10 minutes and let the game begin! Students with flashcards attempt to sell each one for as much money as they can get. Students with money attempt to buy as many flashcards as they can.

Alert the students when there is 2 minutes left in order to encourage a late flurry of activity. When the

2 minutes is up, declare two winners: the student with the most flash cards, and the student with the most money.

It may take the kids a little while to catch on and many are prone to making early financial mistakes, so for these reasons, and because the kids love it, I usually play this game twice.

6. What's your name?

Language / Skill practiced: What's your name / my name is...

Time: 15 minutes

Language level: Beginner to elementary

Have one student come to the front of the class and sit with her back to the class. Point to another student and ask, "What's your name?" This student replies with either his real name or the name of another student, "My name is....."Now ask the student at the front, "Is it (name)?" to which they respond either "Yes, it is" or "No, it isn't." If they answer correctly they go back to their seat, and the student who said, "My name is..." comes to the front of the class to sit facing away from the class and to continue the game. If the student at the front answers incorrectly, they stay at the front and you ask another student, "What's your name?" and so on. Encourage the students to use silly voices to disguise their voice and, when everything is running smoothly, get a student to act the part of the teacher, that is, asking the "What's your name?" and "Is it ....." questions.

7. Fingers on the buzzer

Language / Skill practiced: Spelling

Time: 20 minutes

Language level: Elementary to intermediate

Arrange chairs in a semicircle around your desk and put students into pairs. One of each pair sits in a chair and the other stands behind him with her hands upon his shoulders.

The students sitting in the chairs are the buzzers. Every time the students behind them push down on their shoulders, they must make a "buzzzzz" sound. Only the standing student can speak.

Read out words appropriate to the language level of your students. The first team to "buzz" gets an opportunity to spell the word. Remember, the buzzer can not speak, so it is the standing student who spells the word. Award one point for a correct answer and minus one point for incorrect answers. After 10 minutes or so, swap the students around so that the buzzer gets a chance to speak and spell some words.

Great fun, as the "buzzers" often buzz by mistake when they think they have been pushed, and so on.

8. Pin the tail on the donkey

Language / Skill practiced: Prepositions / directions

Time: 15 minutes

Language level: Elementary to Intermediate

This classic parlor game can be a lot of fun in the ESL classroom. You need two outlines of a tailless donkey, which are fairly easy to construct from card, and two separate tails along with some sticky tack. Set a time limit of one minute or whatever you feel is appropriate. Divide the class into two teams and blindfold a student from each team. Spin them around and issue them both a tail and some sticky tack. Each team must shout instructions to their blindfolded team mate so that he can first, get to the donkey! and then put the tail in the correct place. For example, "fowards..yes..ok..no..left..go left..ok…it's infront of you…up, up, down..stick it there! Yes." The team which gets closest wins a point and it is then the turn of two new students.

9. Blind student hunt

Language / Skill practiced: Directions / listening

Time: 20 minutes

Language level: Elementary to Intermediate

Either push tables and chairs to the side or have them arranged in a kind of maze around the room. Divide the class into two or more teams and pick a student from each team to blindfold and spin around. Now, place an object such as a tennis ball or a mug (you can show this to the students just before they are blindfolded or tell them what it is afterward) somewhere on the floor. Each team has to direct their blindfolded teammate to the object. So language such as, "go forwards, turn left, to the left, pick up," and so on. The first team to pick up the object, wins! Alternatively you can have several objects on the floor and the team who picks up the most, wins. A lot of fun, but I find I have to be very strict on the use of students' native language, taking away points if necessary.

10. What's the time, Mr Wolf?

Language / Skill practiced: Telling time / numbers

Time: 15 minutes

Language level: Beginners to elementary

This classic kids' game works very well in the ESL classroom with younger children. One student plays the part of the wolf and faces the wall at one end of the classroom. The other students stand at the other end of the classroom and call out in unison, "What time is it Mr. Wolf?" The wolf turns and responds with a time such as, "It's six o'clock" before facing the wall once more while the other students move forwards six paces. They then ask again, "What time is it Mr. Wolf?"Again the wolf turns and responds with a time such as, "Its two o'clock" and the other students move forwards two paces. And so on. At some point though, when the students are getting close to the wolf, the wolf will make his move and respond to the student's usual question with, "It's Dinner Time!" he then runs after the other children and if he can "tag" one before they reach the far wall, he or she becomes the wolf. And the game continues…

11. Question catch

Language / Skill practiced: Question forms

Time: 10 to 15 minutes

Language level: Beginner to elementary

Write the question words, "What," "Who," "Where," "When," "How" and "Why" on the board.

Arrange your students in a circle. Throw the ball to one of the students and call out one of the question words, for example, "What." The student who has caught the ball must make a question from this word, for example, "What do you like doing?" and then throw the ball to another student who answers the question, for example, "I like learning English." Call out another question word for this student who makes another question and throws the ball to another student. Allow no repetition of questions so that the game becomes progressively harder and harder.

Options: if you choose, you can eliminate students who cannot think of a question in an appropriate time frame, say 5 seconds, and ask them to sit down until you have a winner. You can also allow the students to choose their own question words to make it a little easier.

12. Vocabulary chairs

Language / Skill practiced: Listening

Time: 10 to 15 minutes

Language level: Beginner to upper-intermediate

This game is a simple adaption of musical chairs, with no music! Arrange the chairs in a circle in the traditional matter so that there is one less chair than there are students. Write on the board some words that you have studied in class or that you wish to revise. For example, you may, after a lesson studying food vocabulary, wish to write the words, "chicken" "carrots" "potatoes" etc. on the board. Now, as the students walk around the chairs, tell them a story (sometimes I prepare a text to read from or, if I haven't had the time, I just make a silly story up featuring the students in the class.) As you are reading the text, slip in words from the board. When the students hear one of the words, they must run to a chair, and the student left standing is out! Continue until you have a winner.

For example,

Teacher: "It was a beautiful day and Sylvia was washing her clothes outside. She heard a barking sound behind her, but when she turned around all she could see was a carrot." (At this point if they are paying attention, the students should rush to their chairs leaving one person standing.)

I like to play a few games of this so that several people have a chance of winning. I also tweak the chair arrangements a little, leaving some big gaps between some of the chairs, so that I can "cheat" a bit and make sure the same student isn't the first out every time.

13. Treasure hunt

Language / Skill practiced: Prepositions of place

Time: 20 to 30 minutes

Language level: Beginners to elementary

This one takes a little bit of preparation but is a lot of fun for the kids, especially if you have your school's permission to let them out of the classroom and into the school proper. It works best when you have a small class, but if you have a large class, then you'll need to prepare 2 or more separate sets of clues; you can always reuse the clues for separate classes. A bit of "real" treasure is a good idea too: some small pieces of chocolate or other treats.

Hide the treasure very well somewhere in the classroom or school. Now you need to hide a series of clues, containing prepositions of place, that will lead the students to the treasure. For example, the first clue that you hand them might read, "under the teacher's desk;" the clue you have hidden under your desk might read, "on top of the whiteboard;" the clue you have hidden on top of the whiteboard might read, "in the lobby next to the potted plant on the left;" and so on, until eventually, after 10 to 15 clues, they are led to the loot!

14. Answer me!

Language / Skill practiced: Question forms / sentence structure

Time: 10 to 15 minutes

Language level: Elementary to upper intermediate

Place a chair at the front of the class and ask one of your students to sit in it. The rest of the class direct questions to this student in an attempt to get him to say the word, "Yes" or the word, "No." If, and usually when, they say either of these words it is somebody else's turn to sit in the seat at the front. It's surprisingly difficult to last many questions!

For example,

Student in the seat: "Ok, I'm ready."

Another student: "Do you like football?"

Student in the seat: "I love football."

Another student: "Do you like Real Madrid?"

Student in the seat: "I hate Real Madrid."

Another student: "Do you often watch them?"

Student in the seat: "No! Oh,……"

Teacher: "Well done, three questions! Who's next?"

If you feel the need to bring a competitive element into the game, you could divide the class into teams and award a point for each question answered without using a "yes" or "no." You can also make this game a bit trickier by ruling that "maybe" and "sometimes" are also prohibited.

15. Last letter first

Language / Skill practiced: Vocabulary / spelling

Time: 10 minutes

Language level: Beginner to pre-intermediate

Divide the class into two or three teams. Teams take it in turns to say a word, any word, within five seconds or less, but it must start with the last letter of the previous team's word.

For example,

Teacher: Ok Team Tiger, Grrrrr, you start.

Team Tiger: Um, "Be"

Team Elephant: Oh, "Elephant. Ha."

Team Snake: "Try."

Team Tiger: "Yellow."

Team Elephant: "Over."

Teacher: "Sorry Team Elephant, 'Yellow,' ends with a 'W.'"

Now, if you wish, you can eliminate Team Elephant and continue with Team Tiger and Team Snake until you have a winner. Or, you can just take away one point from team Elephant and let them continue playing after giving a word starting with "W."

If you want to try the game with higher level students, you'll have to make it a bit trickier by insisting that the words must all be within a particular category e.g. food or countries.

16. Student sentences

Language / Skill practiced: Sentence structure / various

Time: 15 minutes

Language level: Beginner to upper-intermediate

Prepare some sentences appropriate to the level of your students. As many as you can be bothered to make really and of varying lengths. Cut these sentences into individual words and stick them on flashcards. This takes a bit of time but they can be reused again and again, so I think it's worth the effort. Divide the class into teams of five, six, seven or eight; the bigger the teams, the harder the game. Give each team a sentence cut into its individual words, with each member of the team holding one word close to their chest so they can not see it. When you shout "go," each member of each team reveals their word and the team attempts to arrange themselves into a line so that the sentence is in the correct order. The first team to do so wins 5 points, the second 3, and so on. Continue for 15 minutes or so or until, as often happens with me, you run out of sentences of the correct length for the teams. To get the most out of this game, I am fairly strict with students speaking English only and take away points for use of their native language.

17. Word hopscotch

Language / Skill practiced: Vocabulary / pronunciation

Time: 20 minutes

Language level: Beginner to upper-intermediate

This is a great game if you have a big enough classroom, or are able to make use of some outside space. With chalk, draw a traditional hopscotch board on the floor (alternatively, use pieces of A4 paper and tape them to the floor.) Now, in each square, write pieces of vocabulary that you would like your students to practice pronouncing. So your grid might look, for country vocabulary, like this:

England

France

Spain

America Australia

Thailand

Paraguay Yemen

Brazil

Oman

Demonstrate yourself by hopping onto the England square and saying the word, then France, then Spain, and then landing with one foot on America and one foot on Australia and saying both words, then Thailand, then Paraguay and Yemen, then Brazil and finally Oman before returning to the start, saying all the words one more time. Let the students have a few goes before drawing an identical grid next to your first one. Now, the races begin! You can either match up individual students or play as a relay with teams.

However you do it, it will be a lot of fun, and any scoring you choose to implement will become incidental.

18. Riddle me this

Language / Skill practiced: Writing / listening / speaking

Time: 15 to 25 minutes

Language level: Intermediate to advanced

Prepare a couple of fun, simple riddles before class.

For example,

"If you drop me, I'm sure to crack but give me a smile and I'll always smile back. What am I?"

Answer: a mirror.

Or,

"What can you catch but not throw?"

Answer: a cold.

After you've asked the class a few of these, and they have the idea, divide them into groups of three or four to write two or three riddles of their own. After 15 minutes, or when everybody has finished, ask the teams to take it in turns to read their riddles and invite the class to try and guess the correct answer.

19. How are you feeling?

Language / Skill practiced: Feelings vocabulary (+acting!)

Time: 15 minutes

Language level: Beginner to intermediate

This activity requires some basic acting skills on the parts of your students! They soon get the idea if you demonstrate first, and it can be a very funny 15 minutes or so.

Divide the class into teams and have the students come up, in turn, to do a bit of acting at the front. As the student comes up, hand her a slip of paper on which you have written an emotion appropriate to the level of the class. For example, "angry," "happy," "sad" or "interested." They must now act out this emotion to the class. They can make sounds, but no words or it becomes too easy. The first person to guess the emotion wins a point for their team.

20. Steady heads

Language / Skill practiced: Vocabulary / imperatives

Time: 10 minutes

Language level: Beginner to pre-intermediate

Ask students to stand up and give each one a paper cup which they must balance on their head. Issue a series of instructions that the students must follow, for example, "touch your nose," "smile," "bend your knees," "stand on one leg" etc. When a students cup falls from his or her cup, he or she is eliminated from the game. Continue with more instructions until only one student remains, the winner!

21. Countdown

Language / Skill practiced: Vocabulary / spelling

Time: 20 to 25 minutes

Language level: Elementary to advanced

If you are British, then you already know the show on which this activity is based; the activity is very similar to the show. Prepare some flashcards before the lesson with a letter on each one. I have around 80 flashcards with consonants on them and another 30 with vowels on, and that seems to work quite well. Keep the consonants and vowels in separate piles. Divide the class into teams of three or four. Choose one team to begin. They, one by one, choose a combination of nine consonants and vowels. As they choose either a consonant or a vowel, take a card from the appropriate pile and stick it to the board or wall.

For example,

Students: "Consonant, please."

Teacher: (Picks the top card from the consonant pile and sticks it on the board) "T."

Students: "Consonant."

Teacher: (Picks the top card from the consonant pile and sticks it on the board) "S."

Students: "Vowel, please teacher."

Teacher: (Picks the top card from the consonant pile and sticks it on the board) "I."

And so on until there are 9 letters. Start the clock! Students have 60 seconds (the show on TV does 30 seconds, but I've found a minute is better in the classroom) to think of the longest word they can using the letters on the board. So, for example, let's say the letters were: T S I E S R P O K

After a minute stop the students and ask them how long their words are.

Team one: "Um, five letters."

Team two: 'Four letters."

Team three: "Seven."

Teacher: "Ok let's hear the four letter word, Team two."

Team two: "Poke."

Teacher: "Ok, good. Team one?"

Team one: "Tires."

Teacher: "Very nice. And the seven letter word?"

Team three: "Strikes."

Teacher: "Excellent. Seven points to team three. Ok, team two, your turn to pick the letters."

And repeat for four or five rounds.

22. A day at the races

Language / Skill practiced: Past simple / present perfect

Time: 20 to 25 minutes

Language level: Pre-intermediate to intermediate

Before the lesson think of a list of prompts in the past simple or present perfect. I use prompts like, "Things you did yesterday," "Things you have done that you didn't enjoy," "Things you've done that you did enjoy," "Things you did on your last holiday."

Divide the class into two teams and ask them to form two lines facing the board. Divide the board into two halves; one team will write on the left, the other on the right. Give the students at the front of each line a board marker. Tell the students the prompt, for example, "Things you did yesterday." When you shout, "Go" the two students with the pens run to the board and write a short sentence on the board. For example, "I went to school," or "I ate breakfast," or "I saw a movie" etc. When they have written, they run back to their team, give their pens to the students at the front of the line and they themselves move to the back of the line. The new students with the pens run to the board and write their sentences and so on.

After two minutes stop the activity and award each team a point for each correct sentence. (Remember to subtract points for spelling mistakes, tense mistakes and so on.) Repeat with a new prompt until you have completed all your prompts and then declare a winner.

23. Spin the bottle

Language / Skill practiced: Fluency

Time: 15 minutes

Language level: Elementary to advanced

Seat yourself and your students in a circle on the floor with an empty (plastic!) bottle in the middle. Spin the bottle, whoever the top ends up pointing at must answer your question. It is then this student's turn to spin the bottle and ask a question of whomever the bottle ends up pointing at. And so on.

With higher level students, encourage the students to be as creative as possible.

With lower levels, emphasis that they can ask any question, but don't expect much beyond, "Where do you live?" "What do you like?" etc. This is absolutely fine; Rome wasn't built in a day, and they are using the language they possess communicatively.

24. As…..as…….

Language / Skill practiced: Comparisons

Time: 20 minutes

Language level: Pre-intermediate to upper-intermediate

Elicit 15 or so adjectives from your students. For example, "tall," dangerous," "handsome," "ugly," "long," "black" and so on. Write these on the board. For higher level students try and elicit more abstract adjectives in order to make the activity appropriately challenging. Put the class into groups of three or four to construct three phrases comprised of as + adj + as + noun. For example, "As handsome as Pedro," "As long as this English lesson," "As tall as a lighthouse" and so on.

Now each group takes it in turns to read the second half of their phrases for the other teams to guess the adjective.

For example,

Group one: "as a crocodile."

Group two: "ugly?"

Group one: "No..."

Group three: "as dangerous as a crocodile?"

Group one: "Yes, that's right."

Teacher: "Ok, group two. What's your first phrase?"

You can introduce a scoring system if you wish, but I rarely find it necessary.

25. Parts of speech elimination

Language / Skill practiced: Listening / parts of speech

Time: 20 minutes

Language level: Elementary to upper-intermediate

Prepare big pieces of, preferably laminated, card on which you have written parts of speech appropriate to the level of your class. So, for an elementary class I would have cards with the words, "Nouns," "Verbs." "Adjectives" and "Pronouns" on them. For an upper-intermediate class, I would have these cards, as well as ones displaying parts of speech such as gerunds, coordinating conjunctions, reflexive pronouns and so on. Put these pieces of card on the floor scattered around the classroom. Now call out a word, for example, "go." Students have five seconds to run to the appropriate card, in this case, "Verb" and stand on or near it. Those who have run to the wrong card, or are too slow, are eliminated from the game. Continue with a new word until you have winner.

26. Lip Reading

Language / Skill practiced: Vocabulary / pronunciation (kind of!)

Time: 10 minutes

Language level: Beginner to advanced

Bring one student to the front of the class and show them a slip of paper on which you have written a word or sentence appropriate to their language level. The student at the front of the class mouths this word to the rest of the class who try and work out what it is. Repeat with new students.

If you wish you can divide the class into groups in order to play this game competitively with groups who manage to guess the word / sentence receiving points for doing so.

27. Take a pace forwards if you…

Language / Skill practiced: Listening

Time: 20 minutes

Language level: Beginner to pre-intermediate

Have all the students at one end of the room. Now call out instructions, starting with, "Take a step forwards if…" based on whatever you want to practice. For example, "Take a step forwards if you are wearing shorts," to practice clothes; "Take a step forwards if you are wearing a red t-shirt," to practice clothes and colors; "Take a step forwards if you like mushrooms," to practice food; "Take a step forwards if you have fair hair," to practice appearances. Check that no one is cheating, and then call out your next instruction. The first student to reach the far wall, wins.

Repeat two or three times with a student calling out the instructions and you participating in the game. They seem to take a perverse delight in ensuring that you do not win.

28. Blind man's questions

Language / Skill practiced: Listening / question forms

Time: 10 minutes

Language level: Beginner to elementary

Have the students stand in a circle with one student in the middle. Put a blindfold on the student in the middle and spin him around a couple of times. This student then stretches his arm out straight in front of him so that it is pointing at one of the students in the circle. He then asks this student a question—any question, apart from,"What is you name?" For example, "What's your favorite color," or, "Which is your favorite Pokemon?" The student he is pointing at must answer the question, but is allowed to disguise her voice. The blindfolded student must then guess who answered the question. If he guesses correctly then the student who answered the question now becomes the one blindfolded. If he guesses incorrectly, spin him round once more!

29. Play time

Language / Skill practiced: Writing

Time: approx 45 minutes

Language level: Pre-intermediate to advanced

Divide the class into groups of three and give each group a place, a prompt and a line of dialogue. For example,

Place: In a butcher's

Situation: Someone is angry

Line of dialogue: "But I can't come back later!"

Or

Place: In a Park

Situation: Someone has lost something

Line of dialogue: "Of course, I'll phone him right now."

Students now have to prepare a short skit with approximately 10 lines of dialogue, one of which must be the line of dialogue you have given them. Give them approximately 15 minutes to do this. Circulate as they are working on their dialogue and help with any language problems. Try not to help with ideas of how to work the line of dialogue you have given them into the skit though, if possible. Students should then practice their dialogue for another 15 minutes. After the 15 minutes is up, the students should perform their dialogue to the class, without their scripts if possible. As a class, vote for the most realistic dialogue.

30. What's the question?

Language / Skill practiced: Question forms / tenses

Time: 10 minutes

Language level: Pre-intermediate to upper-intermediate

Demonstrate first by writing an answer on the board such as, "When I was ten." Now ask the students, "What's the question?"

For example,

Teacher: "Ok, What's the question?'

Student 1: 'When were you born?"

Teacher: "What? No, Mario…"

Student 2: "When did you learn to ride a bike?"

Teacher: "Good, but no. When I was about six."

Student 3: "When were you learn to swim?

Teacher: "Um, try again."

Student 3: "When did you learn to swim?"

Teacher: "When I was ten. Well done."

Now ask each student to write an answer to an imaginary question and put them in pairs to answer, "What's the question?" After two minutes or when everyone has guessed the question, swap pairs. Continue to swap pairs three more times.

31. Airplane quiz

Language / Skill practiced: Various

Time: 10 minutes

Language level: Elementary to upper-intermediate

Demonstrate to your students, step-by-step, how to make a paper airplane. There are some cool designs on the Internet if you want to make something non-traditional.

Students now make their own paper airplanes. You can award points for the best one if you like. Now, divide the class into teams of three or four and draw a huge target on the board with 100 points at the center, 75 around that, 50 around that and so on. Invite the first team to throw their airplanes at the target. The highest number they manage to hit will dictate how many points they are playing for. If they miss the target completely, you can have them play for 5 points or some smaller amount. Now, ask the group a question. Depending on the needs of the group I might ask vocabulary questions, grammar questions, a spelling question; it really depends on what you would like the focus to be. If they answer correctly then they are awarded the number of points their airplane hit; if they miss, nothing. Move on to the next group. When you have asked all your questions and each team has had an equal amount of turns, tally up the points and announce a winner.

32. Vocabulary race

Language / Skill practiced: Vocabulary / reading

Time: 10 minutes

Language level: Beginner to elementary

Prepare two sets of flashcards containing whichever pieces of vocabulary you would like to practice. For each flashcard with a word on it there should be a corresponding flashcard with a picture on it depicting that word. So you will have two sets of both pictures and words.

At one end of the classroom, pin or stick the picture flashcards to the wall, one set to the left, and one set to the right. Divide the class into two teams and ask each team to stand in a row at the other end of the classroom facing their set of pictures. Place a set of word flashcards facedown in front of each row of students. When you shout "Go," the first student in each row must take a card from the top of the pile and run to the opposite end of the room to stick or pin this word on the correct picture. They then run back to their team and go to the back of the row. The next student in the line can now take a card, run to the other end of the room and stick her word to the correct picture. And so on. When one team has finished, stop the game. Award the team to finish first, 5 points but examine the cards carefully before declaring a winner; for every card placed on an incorrect picture, subtract one point. Also subtract one point for any picture that does not have a word on it. Only then, declare a winner and award a prize if you have one!

33. Can you ball

Language / Skill practiced: "Can you?" questions and answers / pronunciation

Time: 5 minutes

Language level: Beginner to elementary

This is a very good activity to practice the different pronunciations of, "can." Drill the difference in pronunciation of, "can" in a question and, "can" in a short answer exhaustively before you begin.

Students stand or sit in a circle. Ask a "Can you..?" question, for example, "Can you swim?" and throw the ball to another student who responds, "Yes, I can" or, "No I can't." This student then asks a different "Can you..?' question and throws it to another student. And so on. Unlike during other activities, you may wish to stop the students and correct them if their pronunciation is way off mark. You don't really want to reinforce mistakes.

34. Wastepaper bin basketball

Language / Skill practiced: Revision / various

Time: 5 to 10 minutes

Language level: Beginner to advanced

Divide the class into teams of three or four and give each team a sheet of wastepaper which they crumple up into a ball. Place a wastepaper bin at an acceptable distance from the students – not too hard but somewhat challenging; it's no fun if they score every time. Each team has a shot at the basket. The teams that score have an opportunity to answer a question to earn a point for their team. It's up to you what questions you ask. It could be vocabulary, comprehension or whatever. I like to use this activity at the end of a lesson to revise things we have studied that day or to use it at the beginning of the lesson to revise things we studied in the previous lesson.

35. Alphabet statues

Language / Skill practiced: Letters / the alphabet

Time: 10 minutes

Language level: Beginner

Divide the class into teams of four or five. Call out a letter of the alphabet. The students, in their groups, try and arrange themselves into the shape of this letter; they can do this standing up or, if they choose, on the floor. Award points for the best representation of the letter.

36. Play dough numbers and letters

Language / Skill practiced: Numbers / letters

Time: 5 to 10 minutes

Language level: Beginner

This activity is a very basic one for the younger learners. Give every child a piece of play dough. Call out a letter or number and ask them to make that letter or number with their play dough. You can even do short, simple words such as "yes," "no," "dog," and "cat."

37. Body swatting

Language / Skill practiced: Body parts vocabulary

Time: 10 minutes

Language level: Beginner to elementary

Before class draw a large picture of a human body. Stick this to the wall. Divide the class into two lines facing the wall. Give the student at the front of each line a fly-swatter. Call out a body part. The students have to run to the picture and hit the appropriate body part. They then give the fly-swatter to the next student in the line while they themselves go to the back of the line to await their next turn. You can make this activity competitive if you choose, but I've never really felt the need. They seem to just get enjoyment out of hitting the picture!

38. Past tense pelmanism

Language / Skill practiced: Past simple

Time: 20 to 30 minutes

Language level: Elementary to pre-intermediate

Prepare several sets of cards, 20 pairs per set. On one of each pair write a verb appropriate to the level of your students, and on the other card of each pair write the past tense. You need ten cards with verbs on them and ten cards with their past tenses on.

Divide the class into groups of three or four. Place a set of cards, face down in front of the students, spread out over the table. Students take it in turns to turn over, one by one, two cards, and read them aloud. If the two cards are a match i.e. a verb and its past tense, then the student keeps the cards and has another go. If they do not match, they are placed back in the same place they came from, and the students attempt to memorize where they are. It is now the next student's turn. The game ends when all the cards have been collected, and the student with the most pairs, wins.

39. Question quiz

Language / Skill practiced: Question forms

Time: 15 minutes

Language level: Elementary to intermediate

A very useful activity that is also a lot of fun due to the buzzer sounds!

Divide the class into teams of four or five. Assign each team a sound for their buzzer. I like animal sounds, so I have one team bark like a dog, another team meow like a cat and so on.

Give the class an answer to a question, for example, "2015." The first team to buzz in with their team's sound have five seconds to give you a grammatically correct question to the answer. In this case, "What year is it?" or "What year comes after 2014?" would both be acceptable. If they do this correctly, their team gets one point. If they do not give you a grammatically correct question, they lose one point. Repeat with a new answer.

40. Word fetch

Language / Skill practiced: Vocabulary / listening / reading

Time: 15 minutes

Language level: Beginner to elementary

Divide your class into two teams and have them stand at one end of the room. Scatter across the floor vocabulary flash cards and picture flash cards. Each card should have on it either a word or a picture of vocabulary you wish to revise. The more vocabulary and picture flashcards you have, the better. I usually use thirty or so. Now simply call out one of the words. The entire class rush forwards in an attempt to locate and grab the card. Whoever grabs the card first, wins one point for their team. Put the card back on the floor, get the students back to their original positions and call out a new word.

41. Animal mime

Language / Skill practiced: Animal vocabulary

Time: 10 to 15 minutes

Language level: Beginner to pre-intermediate

This is a simple, fun game for younger students, or older ones who are good sports. Put the class into teams of three or four. Ask a member of one of the teams to come to the front. Whisper the name of an animal to this student. The student then acts like this animal in front of the class. The first person to guess the animal wins a point for their team. Continue until everybody has had a go at acting and then tally up the scores to declare a winning team.

42. Reading race

Language / Skill practiced: Reading / listening / writing

Time: 15 minutes

Language level: Elementary to pre-intermediate

This is an interesting way to deal with the many comprehension readings that appear in most course books.

Divide the class into groups of three. Have one of the students from each group sit at one end of the classroom; they are the readers. Have another student from each group sit at the opposite end of the classroom; they are the writers. The final student from each group is going to be the runner.

Give the writers a piece of paper and pencil. Give the readers the text from the course book and start the race! The reader reads a sentence, or more if possible, to the runner who races to the other side of the room to tell the writer who writes it down. The runner then runs back to the reader to receive another / more sentence/s and once again runs back to the writer. They continue until the writer has written down the entire text.

Award 10 points to the first team to finish and 8 to the next team and so on. Only announce a winner, however, after you have omitted points for spelling errors, missing words and so on, and after each group of three has answered the comprehension questions about the text.

43. Who has it?

Language / Skill practiced: Question forms / describing people

Time: 15 minutes

Language level: Elementary to upper-intermediate

Ask one of your students to leave the room. While he waits outside, hand another student an object of some kind: a pen, a ring—it really doesn't matter what—which they secrete somewhere on their person. Ask the student who was waiting outside to come back in and ask her, "Who has the <u>object</u>?"

This student must then, in as few Yes / No questions as possible, deduce who has the object. As soon as they make a guess as to who it is, their turn is over and it is somebody else's go. For example:

Teacher: "Ok, come in. Right, who has the cuddly toy?"

Student 1: "Um, Jose, is the person a boy?"

Jose: "Yes, he is."

Student 1: "Ok. Lek, does this person like football?"

Lek: "No, he doesn't."

Student 1: "Mario, Is this person wearing a red shirt?"

Mario: "Yes, he is."

Student 1: "Ok. I'm ready to guess. Is it Michael?"

Students: 'Yes, that's right."

Teacher: "Ok, good. Just 3 questions! Wow. Ok, who's next?"

44. What's this mingle

Language / Skill practiced: Vocabulary / contractions

Time: 15 minutes

Language level: Elementary to pre-intermediate

Ask the students to stand up and move the chairs and tables to the side of the room. Issue each student with a flashcard with a picture of any vocabulary you'd like to practice. Quickly check that each student knows the piece of vocabulary they are holding. Students hold their flash cards in front of them with the picture showing and approach another student. Each student, in turn, asks / answers the question, "What's this?" They then swap flashcards and find a new partner to repeat the process. For example,

(Students are studying rooms in a house)

Student 1: "What's this?"

Student 2: "It's a bedroom. What's this?"

Student 1: "It's a bathroom"

Students now swap flashcards and find new partners.

or

(Students are studying food)

Student 1: "What's this?"

Student 2: "Um, no idea."

Student 1: "It's a slice of pizza."

Student 2: "A slice of pizza? Oh, ok, thanks. What's this?"

Student 1: "It's a Kebab?"

Student 2: "That's right!"

Students now swap flashcards and find new partners.

45. What's missing flashcards

Language / Skill practiced: Vocabulary / pronunciation

Time: 5 minutes

Language level: Beginner to elementary

Place 10 flash cards with pictures of vocabulary you would like to practice, facedown on the table. Go over the vocabulary, checking pronunciation and meaning. Ask your students to close their eyes; no cheating! Remove one of the pieces of vocabulary. Ask students to open their eyes and tell you which flash card is missing. Repeat.

46. You're joking!

Language / Skill practiced: Reading / jokes

Time: 30 minutes

Language level: Pre-intermediate to advanced

This is a fun activity that almost always proves a hit. Prepare a list of jokes before class, about 15 or so. These jokes should be as simple as possible, humor is very difficult to translate! You can find plenty on line, but here are a few to get you going.

Q: What's brown and sticky?

A: A stick

Q: Which month has 28 days?

A: All of them!

Q: Who do dogs get Christmas presents from?

A: Santa Paws

Cut them into questions and answers and give a set to each group of three or four students to match the questions and answers for each joke. When everyone has finished ask your students which jokes they like, and why. Explain any jokes that the students didn't understand.

Now give the kids, in their groups, five to ten minutes to translate one or more jokes from their native language into English. When they have finished, ask them to tell their jokes to the class.

47. Words worms

Language / Skill practiced: Vocabulary

Time: 5 minutes

Language level: Beginner to elementary

Pick some vocabulary that you have been studying in class and write it as a long string of letters on the board, for example, "easyrunlongalmosthighthoughniceenormouslowlovelydirtydifficultsmallsomebig." Put the class into teams of three or four. The first team to write down all of the words and read them to you correctly, wins.

48. Describe it!

Language / Skill practiced: Vocabulary / describing things

Time: 20 minutes

Language level: Intermediate to advanced

For this activity you need a cardboard box that can close properly and a hole cut in it just big enough for a student's hand to reach inside. Have a number of objects hidden under your desk somewhere where the student's can't see them. Divide the class into groups of three or four. Place an object in the box and ask one student to come to the front and place his hand into the box to feel the object. The rest of the class now asks questions about the object in order to try and guess what it is. But they should not guess yet.

For example,

Class members: "What does it feel like?"

Student: "It feels hard."

Class members: "What shape is it?"

Student: "Round."

Class members: "Is it smooth?

Student: "Yes, it's smooth, but it has a kind of hole in it."

Class members: "Is it heavy?"

Student: "Not heavy, not light"

Class members: "Do you know what it is?"

Student: "I think so."

Class members: "What color do you think it is?"

Student: "Maybe green?"

Teacher: "Ok. enough, write down your answers."

Each group now writes down what they thing it is and holds up their answer. (Make sure the student with his hand in the box doesn't try and mouth the word to his team.) Award a point for the team who has the right answer.

49. Reported speech ball toss

Language / Skill practiced: Reported speech

Time: 10 minutes

Language level: Intermediate to advanced

Arrange the students into a circle. Say a sentence such as, "My name is Miles," and toss the ball to a student. This student must now report what you said, "He said that his name was Miles," and utter a new sentence, perhaps, "What are you doing on the weekend?" before tossing the ball to another student who reports this speech and says a new sentence. And so on. With most classes you will want to limit the game a little to perhaps four or less tenses, or you might want to exclude questions. It all depends on the level of your group and what you have been studying.

50. I don't agree!

Language / Skill practiced: Fluency

Time: 15 minutes

Language level: Intermediate to advanced

Designate one corner of the room: "I agree," another as: "I disagree," another as: "I strongly agree," and the final corner, "I strongly disagree." Call out a statement appropriate to the level and age of your students. For example, "This country should host the Olympics," or "School should be optional."

Now ask the students to move into the corner of their choice and give them five minutes to tell each other why they have chosen that particular corner. When the five minutes are up, mix the groups up so that there is, as far as possible, a person from each corner in each group. Again ask the students to explain their point of view and answer any questions others in the group might have. Repeat, if you wish, with a new statement.

51. Last day word hunt

Language / Skill practiced: Vocabulary review / scan reading

Time: 20 minutes or so

Language level: Elementary to upper-intermediate

This is a nice activity for the last day of class, or the day before if the last day of class will have a test of some kind. Prepare a list of approximately 20 questions related to vocabulary that you have studied during the course. This vocabulary must be in their coursebooks, and you should note down the page number it appears on, or chapter it appears in. Arrange the class into groups of three or four. Make sure that they have their course books in front of them.

Read the first question, for example, "Which word on page 16 means 'very angry'?" or "Which word in Chapter 3 means the opposite of 'generous'?" The students flick to the appropriate page or chapter, and the first person to give you the correct answer wins one point for her team. In these cases, the answers were "furious" and "mean." Continue until you have asked all your questions and declare one team the winners!

52. Show me the time

Language / Skill practiced: Telling time

Time: 20 minutes

Language level: Elementary

Draw the outlines of two clocks on the board, complete with numbers. Arrange the class into two teams in two lines facing the board. Give the two children at the front of each line a pen. Call out a time. The two children run to the board and draw the hands of the clock to represent the time you called out. The first one to do this correctly wins one point for his team. Repeat with the next pair of students and continue until every one has had a go. Tally up the scores and announce a winner.

53. Three part sentences

Language / Skill practiced: Reading / listening

Time: 10 minutes

Language level: Elementary to pre-intermediate

Prepare some sentences on slips of paper, containing language you have been studying in class, and of approximately 20 words in length. You need one sentence for every three people in the class. If you've been studying the past tense you might choose sentences like, "It was an extremely cold day so we decided to put on lots of warm clothes when we went out." or "Mark was trying to get to sleep when he heard a strange noise coming from somewhere in the cold dark house." Now cut these sentences into three parts. (If, as is likely, you can't divide the number of students by three exactly, cut one sentence into either four parts, or two sentences into just two parts.) Ask the students to stand up, push the tables to the side and come to the center of the room. Issue each student a slip of paper and explain that they have one third of a sentence and that they must find the other two thirds. Students read their sentences to each other until they are able to find their partners. When everyone is in their threes (or fours or twos) ask each group to read their sentences to the class.

54. Vocabulary battleships

Language / Skill practiced: Vocabulary / spelling

Time: 10 minutes

Language level: Elementary to pre-intermediate

Issue each child a simple grid with letters on the x axis and numbers for the y axis. Alternatively have them make their own. Ask them to find, from their course book, five words that were new to them before starting the course. Ask them to write these words somewhere in the grid using one letter per cell.

Put students into pairs and ask them to take it in turns to call out coordinates on their partners grid. Their partners will answer with either "miss" for a blank cell, or "hit" if their opponent hits a letter. If their opponent hits a letter they must also say the letter and allow their opponent to keep calling out coordinates until they miss. The first person to hit all the letters of all five words, wins.

55. Animal heads

Language / Skill practiced: Yes / no questions and answers

Time: 10 minutes

Language level: Pre-intermediate to upper-intermediate

This is basically an adaption of the, "Who am I?" game but using animals instead. Begin by writing on the board, "Do not say the name of the animal!" Then write down the names of animals on post it notes and stick one to the forehead of each of your children so that others can see the name of the animal, but the student can not. (What may well happen here is that the kids start saying the names of the animals, so you'll have to point to the board and begin again, so be prepared for this!)

Students circulate, asking each classmate one, "Yes / No" question to try and work out what the animal stuck to their forehead is. They are NOT allowed to ask, however, the question, "Am I a **name of animal**?" When each student has asked their questions, stop the activity and ask each student to tell the class which animal they think they are.

56. Card sentences

Language / Skill practiced: Sentence structure

Time: 15 to 20 minutes

Language level: Intermediate to advanced

Assign each card (regardless of suit) two letters and write these on the board. So, Ace = a b, King = c d and so on. Divide the class into groups of three or four and give each group a deck of cards. Students place the deck of cards face down on the table. They then take it in turns to take a card from the top of the deck and say two words starting with the letters assigned to each card in order to collectively make a long sentence.

For example,

Student 1 (picks a k) : "Can dogs"

Student 2 (picks a ten=i j) : "in jumpers"

Student 3 (picks a ace) : "and bells…."

and so on.

Each group can themselves decide when they must end a sentence and start again. Ask each group to write down some of their longer sentences.

As long as sentences are grammatically correct and make some kind of sense, they are allowed! Stop the activity after 15 to 20 minutes and ask each group to read out their longest sentence.

57. Alphabet Tracing

Language / Skill practiced: Letters / the alphabet

Time: 5 minutes

Language level: Beginner

A very simple activity for absolute beginners. Simply trace letters in the air with your finger and ask your students to tell you what the letter is.

58. Musical words

Language / Skill practiced: Vocabulary / reading

Time: 10 to 15 minutes

Language level: Beginner to elementary

Seat the class in a circle, preferably on the floor. Play some music. Give the students a flashcard with a piece of vocabulary that you wish to revise written on it. Students pass the card around the circle. When you stop the music, the student holding the card must say the word, loudly and clearly. Start the music again and let the students pass the card around once more. When they can all accurately pronounce the first word, I like to introduce a second card, then a third until the class is passing around five or six flashcards to be read out when the music stops.

59. Duck duck goose

Language / Skill practiced: Vocabulary / pronunciation

Time: 15 minutes

Language level: Beginner / elementary

Another traditional game which can work well in the ESL classroom for younger students. You can use whatever vocabulary you wish; it doesn't have to be duck and goose! During one game I tend to change the vocabulary a lot, so that we can cover lots of different words that we have been studying.

Students sit in a circle. The teacher walks around the circle tapping each student in turn on the shoulder saying, "duck…duck…duck" until finally she taps one on the shoulder and says, "goose," at which point she runs around the circle with the goose in hot pursuit. If the goose manages to tag her, she must once again walk around the circle tapping people on the shoulder. If however she manage to get the the child's place in the circle and sit down, it is that child's turn to walk around the circle tapping people on the shoulder, saying, "duck...duck...duck."

60. Preposition commands

Language / Skill practiced: Listening / prepositions of place

Time: 5 to 10 minutes

Language level: Beginner to pre-intermediate

Divide the class into groups of four or five. Move the chairs to the side of the room and have each group stand around a table. Now start barking out instructions to the teams, issuing a point to to the quickest team to follow each instruction. For example, "Get under the table," "Sit on the table," "Stand behind the table," "Get next to the table on my left" and so on. Tally up the points at the end and declare a winner.

61. True / false line

Language / Skill practiced: Vocabulary / pronunciation

Time: 10 minutes

Language level: Beginner / elementary

Tape a line down the middle of the classroom and designate one side as, "True" and the other side as "False." Ask the students to stand in a row astride the line. Hold up a flashcard with a picture of vocabulary you would like to practice on it. Say the word on the card, or a completely different word. Students must jump to either the, "True" side of the line or the "False" side of the line according to whether you are saying the word on the flashcard or not. If you wish, you can eliminate players who jump to the wrong side of the line. Alternatively, you can eliminate the last student to jump to the wrong side of the line. Or you can just play for fun. Continue with more vocabulary flashcards.

62. Spelling Bee

Language / Skill practiced: Spelling

Time: 15 minutes

Language level: Beginner to advanced

Divide the class into teams of three or four and have each student, in turn, come to the front to spell words you assign them. Each correct spelling wins a point for their team. Alternatively, you may wish to have each team elect a speller from their team to perform the tasks. Regardless, when doing this activity with individuals coming to the front, you should tailor the words somewhat to each individual student. Remember the activity is supposed to be rewarding, not humiliating. An alternative method that I often use is to allow each team to confer on the words for 20 seconds or so before producing an answer; this way any blame is shared between several students.

63. How are you?

Language / Skill practiced: Everyday questions and answers

Time: 5 minutes

Language level: Beginner

Good activity for a Monday morning to get students out of their seats and speaking English straight away. Teach / revise four responses to the question, "How are you?" Write these on the board. I use "Fine thanks," "Not too bad, thanks," "Not so great" and "I'm great."

Students stand up and as quickly as possible ask five people "How are you?" As soon as they have finished they can sit down again.

Alternatively, for higher level students, vary the question and do not provide answers on the board. "What did you do on the weekend?" is great for practicing the past simple tense and an apt question for a Monday morning.

64. Close your eyes

Language / Skill practiced: Question forms

Time: 10 minutes

Language level: Elementary to intermediate

Ask one of the students in the class to look closely at an object / piece of furniture / picture / person in the room for 30 seconds. Then ask this student to close her eyes. The other students in the class now fire questions at her. For example, "What color shirt is he wearing?" "Is his pen in his hand?" "Is he wearing a watch? Etc. etc. If the student can keep answering correctly for 2 minutes, he wins a round of applause. Repeat.

65. Yes / no picture cards

Language / Skill practiced: Yes / no questions

Time: 15 minutes

Language level: Elementary

Divide the class into groups of four or five and give each group a pile of flashcards containing vocabulary you would like to practice from a particular topic, for example, transport or places or food etc. Place these flashcards face down, in a pile, in front of them.

The object of the game is to collect as many cards as possible. Pick a student from each group to go first. They pick a flashcard from the top of the pile and hold it up, facing them so that the other students can't see it. The other students take it in turns to ask yes / no questions in order to determine what is on the card.

For example, (Topic is countries)

Student 1: "Is it in Asia?"

Student 2: "No, it isn't."

Student 3: "Is it in Europe?"

Student 2: "Yes, it is."

Student 1: "Is it a hot country?"

Student 2: "No, it isn't.'

and so on.

When one of the students think they know what is on the card they can make a guess, for example, "Is it England?"

If they are correct, they get the card; this card represents one point and is now out of play. If they are incorrect, then the student holding the flashcard gets to keep the card; again it represents one point and is now out of play.

Play continues with the student to the left of the original student taking a card from the top of the pile and answering questions about it, as before.

After 15 minutes, stop the activity and ask students to count how many cards they have and declare a winner.

66. Minimal pairs bingo

Language / Skill practiced: Listening

Time: 10 minutes

Language level: Intermediate to advanced

This takes a little preparation but is well worth it as you can simply print out the grids and play again. Pick one or more minimal pairs that your students have been having trouble with such as "i / ee" or "sh/ch" and prepare some five-by-five bingo grids for your students with words featuring these sounds. For example, "ship / sheep," "lip / leap," etc. Demonstrate the concept of bingo to your students if they are not familiar with it and then simply read out words from their grids until somebody has heard all their words and shouts, "Bingo!"

You must, of course, check their grid as it's very easy for students to make mistakes with minimal pairs even at the higher levels.

67. Please listen to me

Language / Skill practiced: Listening / imperatives

Time: 5-10 minutes

Language level: Elementary to pre-intemediate

This activity is much like Simon Says but uses a far greater range of imperatives than simply, "touch." Instruct your students to follow your commands, but only when you say, "please." Eliminate students that fail to do so correctly until you have a winner. Commands can range from, "Please run," to "Please hop," to "Please shout," to "Please lie down." You are only really limited by your students' range of vocabulary.

I like to focus on verbs that we may have studied recently when doing this activity. For example, after studying animals, I might instruct the students to "Please meow," "Please bark like a dog," "Please walk like a chicken" and so on.

68. Dice lottery

Language / Skill practiced: Various / revision

Time: 15 minutes

Language level: Beginner to intermediate

This activity works best with smaller classes. Divide the class into two teams: A and B and give each team a dice. Ask the teams, in turn, questions related to anything you wish to revise or practice, or set them tasks. For example, "What's the opposite of long?" or "Name everything Jose is wearing." A correct answer or response means that they have an opportunity to roll the dice and will receive the number of points they roll, EXCEPT, if they roll a three, in which case the other team gets three points. Continue for 15 minutes or until the students start to lose interest. Tally up the scores and announce a winner.

69. Can you remember?

Language / Skill practiced: Vocabulary

Time: 10 minutes

Language level: Beginner

Place a number of picture flashcards with vocabulary on them which you wish to revise. Invite the students to tell you the names of these things and check pronunciation. Now take the flashcards away and ask the class to tell you all the things that were on the table. Ask several of your students to, individually, tell you the words they remember and remind them of any they missed. Next put students in pairs to tell each other the vocabulary they can remember, and, finally, ask each student to, individually, write down the vocabulary.

After 5 minutes, or when everyone has finished, write the list of words on the board so that students can check their work.

70. Question circle

Language / Skill practiced: Question forms

Time: 15 minutes

Language level: Beginner to pre-intermediate

This is a good activity for practicing common question forms such as, "Do you like + verbing," "Can you + verb" "What time do you + activity" and so on. Have the class sit in a circle. And ask the child to your left a question such as "Do you like swimming?" The student answers, "Yes, I do" or "No, I don't." At this point with lower level student's you might choose to just continue with the same question, so the child turns to the student on her left and asks, "Do you like swimming" and so on around the circle until you ask a new question. Better though, if your students can handle it, is to have them change the verb so that every student asks a new question, but in the same form, such as, "Do you like eating chocolate?" or "Do you like reading?" Continue around the circle for a couple of rotations, before changing the question form if you wish.

71. Describe your classmates

Language / Skill practiced: Describing people

Time: 15 minutes

Language level: Pre-intermediate to Intermediate

Ask each student to write their name on a slip of paper and hand it to you. Shuffle the pieces of paper up and redistribute them to the students under strict instructions to keep the names a secret. Students take it in turns to describe the person on their slip of paper and the rest of the class guess who it is. For example,

"This person is quite tall and has brown hair and, I think, green eyes. He usually wears jeans and a t-shirt........" and so on. The first person to guess who it is, goes next.

Note: Tell your students NOT to look at the person they are describing when they do this activity.

72. Story time

Language / Skill practiced: Sentence structure / parts of speech

Time: 15 minutes

Language level: Pre-intermediate to intermediate

Issue every student a word, appropriate to their language level, on a slip of paper. Instruct them to keep this word a secret.

Tell the class that you are going to tell a story and that each student will contribute a sentence and that that sentence must contain the word they have on their slip of paper. Begin the story yourself (I usually like to include a students name in the first sentence to make it a bit more personal) with a sentence such as , "It was a sunny day and Juliet was walking to the beach" then choose another student to continue the story. After they have said their sentence they choose another student to add the next sentence and so on until everyone has had a go. Write the story on the board as the students are making it and when it is finished ask the class to guess what each student had written on their slip of paper. In addition, use this written record to go over any mistakes and / or especially good sentences.

73. Preposition race

Language / Skill practiced: Prepositions / listening

Time: 20 minutes

Language level: Elementary to intermediate

Prepare a text of a suitable language level for your class. Divide the class into groups of three or four and seat each group an equal distance from your desk. Give each group, on slips of paper, all the prepositions which appear in the text. Now read the text an an appropriate speed but omit the prepositions, replacing them with the word "beep" (or any other word you like). So for example,

Teacher (reading text): "Hilary was the first man to climb Everest, the highest mountain **BEEP** the world."

The first person to place the appropriate preposition on your desk wins one point for their team. Any team who places the incorrect preposition on your desk loses one point. Continue reading the text, replacing prepositions with "BEEP." When you have finished the text, add up the scores and declare a winner.

74. Word morphing

Language / Skill practiced: Vocabulary

Time: 10 minutes

Language level: Elementary to advanced

With higher level classes you can play this game as individuals, but with lower level class it is advisable to divide your class into groups of at least four. Write a four letter word on the board, for example, "make." Each group (or student at higher levels) in turn has to change one letter to make a new word. Set a time limit for each group / student depending on their language level. I usually allow 15 seconds or so once they've got the idea of the activity. If the group / individual can't think of a word in this time, they are out and play continues without them until you have a winner. For example, the word is "Make."

Group 1: Male

Group 2: Made

Group 3: Mode

Group 1: (Can't think of a word: they are out)

Group 2: Mole

Group 3: hole

Group 2:(Can't think of a word: they are out)

Group 3 are the winners!

Repeat for 10 minutes or until students start to lose interest.

75. Seven things

Language / Skill practiced: Vocabulary

Time: 15 to 20 minutes

Language level: Elementary to intermediate

Seat the class on chairs in a circle. Stand outside the circle, or ask a student to. Give one of the students a ball. Give the student sitting to his right a task, starting with, "Name seven …" This task should be related to something you are studying or wish to revise. So if you've just been looking at places, you might say, "Name 7 places in a city." The student with the ball passes it to the student to his left who passes it to the student to her left and so on. The original student must name the seven places before the ball reaches the student on his right. So if, for example, he manages to say, "Post office, Train station, Shop, Cafe, Police station, Park and Vets," before the ball reaches the student on his right, he wins. Reward with a round of applause and repeat with a different student and a different task.

Note: It doesn't have to be seven things, depending on the size of the class you might choose a higher or lower number.

76. Student sit down

Language / Skill practiced: Listening / responding

Time: 10 minutes

Language level: Beginner to upper-intermediate

This game, as well as being thoroughly enjoyable, encourages students to respond quickly, without over-thinking things. Divide the class into two teams and have each team line up facing you.

Ask the two students at the front a question appropriate to their language level. For example, "How are you?" "What's the tallest mountain in the world?" "What did you eat for dinner yesterday?" and so on. The first student who answers correctly, gets to sit down on the floor, or a chair if you wish. The other student goes to the back of his line. You now ask another question to the next two students. The first team to have everyone sitting down, wins!

77. Past, present or future

Language / Skill practiced: Time phrases / fluency

Time: 15 minutes

Language level: Pre-intermediate to upper intermediate

Brainstorm some time-phrases and write these on the board; phrases like, "today," "at the moment," "last week," "2 weeks ago," "these days," "sometimes," "almost always," "on the weekend," "in the last few weeks" and so on. Arrange your students in a circle, or at least ensure everyone knows who is first, second etc. The first student starts by saying a time phrase. The second student uses this in a true sentence and then says a new time phrase, and so on. Ask students not to repeat verbs.

For example,

Student 1: "at the moment"

Student 2: "At the moment, I'm sitting in class. Sometimes."

Student 3: "Sometimes my father likes to eat hamburgers. These days."

Student 4: "These days, it is difficult to find a job. Last week."

Student 5: "Last week, Um.. last week I went to Hai Phong."

Continue for a round or so and then divide the class into smaller groups and ask them to continue the activity in their smaller groups.

78. Slow motion reveal

Language / Skill practiced: Vocabulary

Time: 5 minutes

Language level: Beginner to elementary

Divide the class into teams of four or five. Have a pile of flashcards with pictures of vocabulary you would like to practice on them. Hold up a flashcard for the class, but covered with a sheet of paper or card. Slowly slide down the paper or card to reveal, bit-by-bit, the picture. The first person to say the correct word gains one point for her team. If you wish you can take away points for incorrect answers.

79. That's not true!

Language / Skill practiced: Various / fluency

Time: 15 to 20 minutes

Language level: Pre-intermediate to upper-intermediate

Write some sentences about your class on the board. For example, "Most of the class like football." "Everybody in this class has a brother or sister," "No one in this class was born on November 25" and so on. Students stand up and ask questions of their fellow students e.g. "Do you have a brother or sister?" "When were you born?" and so on in an attempt to disprove as many of the sentences as possible. After 5 minutes stop the activity and ask students to get into groups to pool their findings. After another 5 minutes stop the activity and ask each group to share with the class which statements they have disproved. For example, "Michael doesn't have a brother or a sister," "Christian was born on the 25 December," and so on.

80. Whacky races

Language / Skill practiced: Action verbs

Time: 10 minutes

Language level: Beginner to elementary

A simple but fun game to practice verbs of action. Have the kids stand at one end of the room and then race to the other, but with a twist; instruct them to Hop to the other side of the room, to Jump, to Crawl, to Roll, to Walk, to Run, to Slither like a snake, to Stride like a Giant, to Tiptoe. Indeed any verbs of action you would like to practice.

81. Train ride

Language / Skill practiced: Action verbs

Time: 5 to 10 minutes

Language level: Beginner to elementary

Form the kids into a human train, that is in a line with hands on the hips of the student in front with you at the front. Pull the whistle, "Weeeeee" and move forwards "Choo, choo, choo, choo." From here you can, "turn left," "turn right" "Stop (car coming)," "back up" and so on. There is a surprising amount of vocabulary that you can practice just being a train!

82. Code words

Language / Skill practiced: Spelling / numbers

Time: 10 minutes

Language level: Pre-intermediate to upper-intermediate

Write the letters of the alphabet on the board and under each one put a number: so A = 1, B=2 and so on. Explain how the code works and practice a few as a class. For example 3 1 20 would equal CAT. C=3 1=A 20=T. Now divide the class into groups of three or four and start calling out some words in the number code. The first team to tell you the correct word wins one point for their team.

After five minutes or so, extend the activity by having each group work out some words of their own in number code and call them out for the other groups to guess.

83. Dominoes

Language / Skill practiced: The alphabet

Time: 15-20 minutes

Language level: Beginners

This game is good practice for real beginners who have just learned, or are in the process of learning, the alphabet. Take some time before class to print out some simple dominoes on paper or, preferably, on card. Instead of numbers though, use letters, and if you think your students are up to it, both upper and lower case letters. Play dominoes as you normally would but allow lower / upper-case matches and encourage the kids to say the letters as they place their cards down.

84. Snap-shot hunt

Language / Skill practiced: Vocabulary

Time: 30 minutes

Language level: Elementary to upper-intermediate

This activity is a lot of fun for older children who have access to a camera. Most of my older students seem to have a mobile phone with camera and you only need two or three for this activity, so why not make use of them?

Divide the class into two or three teams and issue each team a list of things you'd like a photo of. Really tailor this list to your class's language level so that there are some words they have to double check, some they know and some they have to look up in a dictionary. For example for a pre-intermediate class I might request pictures of:

1. someone looking perplexed

2. An exotic plant

3. A mouth-watering food

4. A spacious room

5. Someone dressed well.

Send the class of into the wilds of your school building with instructions not to disturb other classes. The first team to return with all the correct pictures, wins.

85. ABC Song

Language / Skill practiced: The alphabet

Time: 5 minutes

Language level: Beginner

I'm sure you're familiar with the ABC song and of course, getting your students to sing along with it is a valuable activity. You can also expand it a little using flash cards with letters of the alphabet on them. Randomly give each student a flashcard and stand them against the wall. As the song plays, when they hear their letter they raise their flashcard. Or, do the same thing but as the song plays have them arrange themselves in the correct order. Or have the students stride around the room as the music is playing and then randomly stop the music; when the music stops they must arrange themselves in an alphabetical line and then call out their letter in sequence.

86. Stand up letters

Language / Skill practiced: Letters / the alphabet

Time: 10 minutes

Language level: Beginner

This is a really simple little game, but the kids seem to love it. Randomly assign each kid a flash card with a letter on it and ask them to sit down on the floor in front of you. Call out a letter. The child who has this card must stand up, say his letter and then sit down again. Repeat with more letters gradually increasing the speed until you are going as fast as possible. Alternatively, instead of saying the letters, use a second set of flash cards and reveal the letters instead.

87. Stand up conditionals

Language / Skill practiced: Conditionals / if clauses

Time: 10 minutes

Language level: Pre-intermediate to intermediate

Seat your students in a circle on chairs, with you in the middle. Issue an instruction in a conditional tense. For example, "If you are wearing red, change seats," "If you like pasta, change seats," "If you have been to Australia, change seats" and so on.

So if, for example, you said the first of the above sentences, any students wearing red must stand up and change seats. They must do this quickly however as you will try and sit in one of their seats as they move. If you manage to sit down then the student left standing issues the next command. If you don't manage to sit down you must issue another command.

88. Tic tac toe pictures

Language / Skill practiced: Vocabulary

Time: 10 minutes

Language level: Beginner to elementary

This game is best played with smaller classes. Draw a tic tac toe grid on the board. In each cell draw a very simple drawing of any vocabulary you would like to practice (If you are a terrible drawer, you can stick flashcards in each cell instead.) Divide the class into two teams: one team is X, the other, O. Each team takes it in turns to pick a drawing and either say the word or, for slightly more advanced classes, come to the board and write the word under the picture. If they do this successfully then you can replace the picture with either an X or an O. The first team to get three in a row, wins.

89. Follow the leader

Language / Skill practiced: Action verbs

Time: 5 to 10 minutes

Language level: Beginner to elementary

A nice way to start or finish a class. Have the kids march behind you as you stride around the classroom. Shout out and demonstrate different actions for the kids to mimic. For example, skip, scratch your head, hop, walk sideways and so on.

90. Kabaddi tasks

Language / Skill practiced: Various

Time: 20 minutes

Language level: Beginner to elementary

Kabaddi originated in the Punjab region of India and is a contact sport popular in much of S. Asia. We'll play the non-contact version, however! The crux of the game is that students must complete tasks while repeatedly saying the word Kabaddi to prove that they are not inhaling; it's an alternative time limit that will differ from student to student.

Prepare a series of tasks for your students; these could be a gap fills, matching exercises or cut up sentences—it's really up to you, and whatever you're studying with your students. Place the tasks on a table in the center of the room.

Divide the class into groups of three or four and ask each group to stand next to the wall some distance from the table. Choose a group to go first. This group selects a champion who must run to the table, all the while saying "KabaddiKabaddiKabaddiKabaddiKabaddiKabaddiKabaddiKabaddi," to prove she is not inhaling, complete as many tasks as she can without drawing breath and return to her group still saying, "KabaddiKabaddiKabaddiKabaddiKabaddiKabaddiKabaddiKabaddi." She then earns as many points as tasks she has completed, and it is another groups' turn. If at any point a student stops saying "kabaddi" while away from her group and performing the task, then no points are awarded to that group for that turn.

Continue until your students have run out of breath!

91. Article Challenge

Language / Skill practiced: Articles

Time: 20 minutes

Language level: Elementary to intermediate

Divide the class into teams of three or four and issue each team with two flash cards. One flash card has "A" written on it, and the other, "An." The game is really simple. You read either sentences with the article omitted such as, "I saw … elephant"; "…good way to study is to read"; "Do you have … pencil," or single words such as "hat" "tiger" "teacher" and so on. The first team to raise the correct flash card wins one point. Any team that raises the incorrect flash card is deducted one point.

Note: If you can find a good way to incorporate, "the" into the game that isn't too complex, well done; you are a better man/woman than me!

92. Traffic Lights!

Language / Skill practiced: Listening / imperatives

Time: 10-15 minutes

Language level: Beginner to elementary

Prepare three large, circular pieces of card: one red, one yellow, and one green. Assign one student the role of traffic lights and give her the pieces of card. Assign another student the role of traffic policeman. The other students in the class should walk around the room. The traffic light student holds up whichever card he likes and issues a command. Red = "Stop," Green = "Go" and Yellow = "Be careful." If the traffic light is green, students can continue walking around the room without fear. If the traffic light is red, students must freeze, and anyone the traffic policeman sees moving, is out of the game. On yellow, students can move if they choose but anyone the policeman sees moving and tags, is out of the game. Continue until only one student, the winner, remains.

93. Mannequin

Language / Skill practiced: Clothes vocabulary

Time: 20 minutes

Language level: Beginner to elementary

This is a really fun and funny activity, but you must have access to lots of clothes. If you are working somewhere semi-reputable, there is a good chance that they will have a bin-full of clothes ready for you to use. Otherwise, if you want to try this activity, you will need to invest a bit of money at a secondhand stall and a laundrette!

Divide the class into two teams and play a quick game of categories (that is, each team takes it in turns to say an item of clothing within five seconds, no repetition. Write down the clothes for each team on the board until each team has six or so items of clothing.) Alternatively, simply list two sets of six items of clothing on the board.

Ask each team to stand up and to elect a shop dummy, or mannequin. Ask the two mannequins to take off their shoes. Tip your bin or bag of clothes on the floor and tell the teams to dress their mannequin with the clothes they listed while the mannequin stays passive i.e. doesn't dress himself.

The first team to successfully dress their dummy with the clothes they listed, wins!

94. Have I made a mistake?

Language / Skill practiced: Various

Time: 15 minutes

Language level: Elementary to advanced

The great thing about this activity is that it can be used for almost any language level. Divide the class into groups of three or four and ask each group to write down 5 sentences on a sheet of paper. Four of the sentences should be grammatically incorrect and only one grammatically correct. If you wish, you can confine your students' sentences to a certain grammatical area, for instance the present perfect or a conditional tense.

Each group now swaps their sheet of paper with another group and attempts to a) identify the grammatically correct sentence (one point) and b) correct the grammatically incorrect sentences (one point for each correctly corrected (!) sentence.)

95. Holiday time

Language / Skill practiced: Going to / present continuous

Time: 10-20 minutes

Language level: Elementary to intermediate

Ask your students to stand up and inform them that you are going on a long holiday to Hawaii, and that some of the students can come with you. Tell them,

"I'm going to Hawaii and I'm taking a (object) with me."

Now, ask the students one-by-one what they are taking with them. If they name an object in the same category, tell them they can come and to sit down. If they name a object that isn't in your category then they remain standing.

So, for example, if you started with, "I'm going to Hawaii and I'm taking a lap-top with me," Students must now say a sentence declaring that they are bringing something electrical, for example, a phone, an ipod, an iron and so on. If you started with, "I'm going to Hawaii and I'm taking a knife with me," then students must name a kitchen utensil, for example a corkscrew, a fork and so on. It will take your students a little while to get the hang of the game but as soon as they do, its a lot of fun and you can then divide them into groups to play on their own.

Let's look at a quick example,

Teacher: "I'm going to Hawaii and I'm taking a cup of coffee with me."

Student 1: "I'm taking a can of coke."

Teacher: "I'm sorry, you can't come. Next."

Student 2: "I'm taking a cup of tea."

Teacher: "Welcome. We will have a great holiday!"

Student 3: "I'm taking some milk."

Teacher: "Oh dear. You can't come."

Student 4: "I'm taking some hot chocolate."

Teacher: "Great!"

And so on. (The object must be a hot drink)

96. Alphabet catch

Language / Skill practiced: The alphabet

Time: 5 minutes

Language level: Beginner

A really simple little activity for students who are learning the alphabet. All you need is a small beanbag. Have your class stand in a circle and say, "A." Toss the ball to another student who must say "B" and throw the bean bag to another student who says, "C" and so on. Increase the speed and start with different letters of the alphabet as the students become more proficient. I like using this as a warmer for my lower level classes as it wakes everyone up and gets their minds into the, "English Zone."

97. Would I lie to you?

Language / Skill practiced: Present perfect / various

Time: 20 minutes

Language level: Pre-intermediate to advanced

Give each student a sheet of paper with five questions on it. It's ok if you repeat questions, but try and get as much variety as possible. Questions should be of a nature that a, "Yes, I have" answer is not impossible.

For example,

"Have you ever been skinny dipping?"

"Have you ever been scuba diving?"

"Have you ever gone 72 hours without sleep?"

"Have you ever drunk beer?"

"Have you ever been in a canoe?"

and so on.

Divide the class into groups of four. One student from each group begins by asking one of their questions to the student on their left to which this student must reply, "Yes, I have."

At this point, any of the other students in the group can ask supplementary questions to determine whether this answer is true.

For example:

Student 1: "Have you ever drunk beer?"

Jose: (on the left): "Yes, I have."

Student 3: "When?"

Jose: "Last week."

Student 1: "Who with?"

Jose: "My dad."

Student 1: "Really? Your dad lets you drink beer? How much?"

Jose: "A bottle."

Student 4: "But you are only 12. Did you like it?"

Jose: "Yes, delicious."

Student 1: OK, thanks I have enough information.

Student 1 now makes a note next to his question such as, "Jose is not telling the truth."

It is now Jose's turn to ask a question to the student on his left and so on until all the questions have been asked and answered.

When everyone has finished, ask the students to re-ask their questions but to answer them honestly.

Students see how many times they guessed correctly whether a student was lying or not. The student in each group who guessed correctly the most times wins.

98. Chinese whispers with a twist

Language / Skill practiced: Listening / vocabulary

Time: 10 minutes

Language level: Beginner to intermediate

Arrange your students in a line. Place five flashcards on the floor with words you'd like to practice written on them. The closer these words sound like each other, the harder the activity will be. So for a strong class, "thin," "thick," "think," "then," and "this" might be appropriate.

Whisper one of these words to the first student in the line who whispers it to the second student and so on, until the final student who must pick the appropriate flashcard from the floor.

Alternately, you can arrange the class into two teams / lines with two sets of flashcards and turn it into a race.

99. Stop Boasting

Language / Skill practiced: Fluency

Time: 15 minutes

Language level: Pre-intermediate to advanced

Put your students into pairs for this activity, after pre-teaching the word and concept, "Boast". Students take in in turns to try and out-brag each other!

For example,

Student 1: "I'm rich."

Student 2: "I'm rich and handsome.'

Student 1: "I'm rich, handsome and intelligent."

Student 2: "I'm so intelligent, I can play chess with my eyes shut."

Student 1: "I learned chess when I was 1 month old. It was very easy."

Student 2: "I learned chess and how to drive a car when I was 1 month old."

Student 1: "I drive a Ferrari."

Student 2: "Someone drives my Ferrari for me."

And so on.

100. Good sentence, bad sentence

Language / Skill practiced: Listening / grammar

Time: 15 minutes

Language level: Beginners to pre-intermediate

Prepare ten or so sentences before class, some of which are grammatically correct and some of which are grammatically incorrect. It is ideal if these are sentences that you heard members of your class utter in the previous lesson. Divide the class into groups of three or four and issue each group with two cards, about A4 size. On one card should be written the word, "Good sentence" and on the other, "Bad sentence." Read the sentences out, one by one. After each sentence give the groups 20 seconds to converse, after which they must raise either their good sentence card or their bad sentence card. Award one point to each team that raises the correct card. If you wish you can also award a point to teams who can correctly correct bad sentences.

101. Musical objects

Language / Skill practiced: Fluency

Time: 20 minutes

Language level: Elementary to intermediate

This activity works better with smaller classes. With classes over about seven students, there's a lot of standing around and listening to other students rather than speaking.

Bring some objects into class; anything you've got lying around really, or that you can scavenge from the teachers' room. For example, a cup, a t-shirt, a tie, an apple, a photograph and so on. Place the same number of chairs as you have students in the middle of the room in a circle. Play some music. The students walk around the chairs in a circle and when the music stops, they stop. Each student must know, in turn, say three or more sentences about themselves and the object in front of them. For example,

Student who stops in front of the mug: I drink coffee from a mug every morning. I need coffee in the morning. If I don't drink coffee, I can't do anything.

Student who stops in front of the T-shirt: I like t-shirts. But I don't like this one. It looks dirty. Is it yours, teacher?

When everyone has spoken, turn the music back on and repeat. The higher the level of student, the more creative you can encourage them to be.

102. Name lines

Language / Skill practiced: Listening / learning classmates' names

Time: Should be 10 to 15 minutes, often much longer...

Language level: Elementary to pre-intermediate

A good, sometimes quick, activity for the first day of class. Ask your students to stand up and put them into groups of four or five. Students ask the classmates in their group their names and then stand in a alphabetic line according to the first letter of their first name. If two or more students in one group have the same first letter in their names, they must use the second letter. So Adam would come after Aaron and so on. If two or more students have the same first and second letter in their name then they must use the third letter in their name. When the students in each group have arranged themselves in a line ask them, in turn, to call out their names so that you can all, as a class, check that they are in the correct order.

Now, create bigger groups by turning two groups into one. So if you originally had four groups you should now have two. Repeat the activity. Keep combining groups and repeating the activity until you have the whole class in one line. By this time, every one should know each other's names as well as having interacted, in English, with their classmates.

Other books by this author

102 ESL Games and Activities for New and Prospective Teachers

Basic English Grammar: A Guide for New and Prospective ESL Teachers

English Grammar Exercises: A Complete Guide to English Tenses for ESL Students

Printed in Poland
by Amazon Fulfillment
Poland Sp. z o.o., Wrocław